ats

S0-DOR-595

ST. MARY SCHOOL
LIBRARY

SATELLITE TECH TALK

By Ruth and Ed Radlauer
Jean and Bob Mather

Cartoons by Eileen Morris

AN ELK GROVE BOOK
CHILDRENS PRESS, CHICAGO

**Created for Childrens Press by
Radlauer Productions, Incorporated**

The authors are grateful to physicist William G. McKinley
for authentication of the manuscript.

Photo credits:
Ford Aerospace, page 4
Jet Propulsion Laboratory, pages 8, 12, 13, 18, 24, 29, 31, 34,
    40, 45, 47, 59, 61, 63
RCA, pages 22, 27, 36, 43, 48, 50, 55
Ruth Radlauer, cover and page 53

Library of Congress Cataloging in Publication Data

Main entry under title:
Satellite tech talk.

   (Tech talk books)
   "An Elk Grove book."
   Summary: A dictionary of words and terms relating to
satellites, from active satellite and aerospace to yaw
and zenith.
   1.   Artificial satellites—Dictionaries, Juvenile.
[1.   Artificial satellites—Dictionaries]   I.   Radlauer,
Ruth Shaw.   II.   Series
TL796.S263   1984   629.47'03'21   83-21059
ISBN 0-516-08253-1

Copyright © 1984 by Regensteiner Publishing Enterprises, Inc.
All rights reserved. Published simultaneously in Canada.
Printed in the United States of America.

1   2   3   4   5   6   7   8   9   10   11   12   13   14   15   R   90   89   88   87   86   85   84

629.8
R-M-S

ST. MARY SCHOOL
LIBRARY

Tech Talk Books

Computer Tech Talk
Radio Tech Talk
Robot Tech Talk
Satellite Tech Talk

86-57

*An ACTIVE SATELLITE, one of 15 INTELSAT communications satellites.
"Wingspan" 50 feet. Weight 400 pounds at launch.*

A

A, the first letter of the alphabet, helps us say A book, A space traveler, and A satellite. A *Satellite **Tech Talk*** book explains many of the important words people use when they talk about, read about, work on, or study satellites. After you read *Satellite Tech Talk*, reread it, and keep it handy, you'll know a lot about those important objects that people put out in space. See *Space*.

An **ACTIVE SATELLITE** is a working satellite. In space, it measures things, compiles the data, computes it, and sends the information back to Earth.

In order for us to see an event that's taking place on the other side of the world, such as the Olympics, an ACTIVE SATELLITE picks up the radio waves from the broadcast in the country where the games are played. The ACTIVE SATELLITE makes the waves stronger (amplifies them), and sends them to ground stations everywhere. The signals can be sent immediately if it has an instantaneous repeater or after a while if it has a delayed repeater. When sent immediately, we can see what's happening as the event takes place. See *Amplification*.

AEROSPACE is the scientific study of the Earth's atmosphere and the space beyond. It is also the name given to the huge industry that builds, designs, and operates the instruments for the many experiments and activities we carry on in the atmosphere and in space. See *Atmosphere.*

AMPLIFICATION makes electrical impulses stronger. An amplifier makes radio waves stronger by AMPLIFICATION. See *Active Satellite, Radio Waves.*

AMPLITUDE is the name for one of the characteristics of a wave. The AMPLITUDE refers to the strength of the wave. The more powerful a wave is, the larger its AMPLITUDE is. The larger the AMPLITUDE of a radio wave is, the louder it sounds to you. The larger the AMPLITUDE of a radio wave, the further away a satellite can be and still communicate with its Earth station. See *Radio Waves, Wave.*

ANALOG COMPUTER You use an ANALOG COMPUTER when you hike with a compass or check your bike-riding speed with a speedometer. An ANALOG COMPUTER uses the change in something, rather than arithmetic, to do mathematics. First the changes have to have numbers to mark the amount of change. Then as changes take place, the numbers are read out. Another example of an ANALOG COMPUTER is a thermometer. The change that takes place in a thermometer is the height of the column of liquid inside the glass tube. Numbers marked on the thermometer give us a mathematical readout. As the temperature goes up or down, the height of the liquid changes, and the readout changes.

Used on a satellite, an ANALOG COMPUTER collects data by measuring changes in things of nature such as the brightness of a light or the temperature of a surface. It sends this data to a digital computer on Earth to be processed into information people can understand. It is not as accurate as the digital computer, but it's much, much faster. See *Computers, Digital Computer* and the book, *Computer Tech Talk.*

ANTENNAS are metal structures that stick out of a satellite's surface. They focus radio waves the way lenses focus light. ANTENNAS are used to control where radio waves go. A satellite picks up data in outer space and sends it to Earth on modulated radio waves. The data might be something like the number of cosmic rays a satellite encounters, the size of the cloud cover on a planet, or the strength of a planet's magnetic field. See *Cosmic Rays, Data, Encounter, Magnetic Field, Modulation, Radio Waves.*

The **APOGEE** of a satellite in orbit is the point at which it is the farthest from the body it is orbiting. See *Orbit, Perigee.*

APOLLO A long time ago the Greeks believed in a god of light named APOLLO. Some versions of the story have APOLLO driving a chariot that pulls the Sun across the sky. Quite a good job for someone who likes sunburn. But now we call something else APOLLO. It's the name for a space mission that put the first human being on the surface of the Moon. In 1969, Astronaut Neil Armstrong stepped out onto the Moon and said, "That's one small step for a man, one giant leap for mankind." The APOLLO crews consisted of three men. See *Gemini, Mercury.*

An **ASTEROID** is a huge body of rock that orbits the Sun. It can be between one mile and 500 miles in diameter. There is a large belt of asteroids between the orbits of Mars and Jupiter. See *Orbit, Planet.*

APOLLO 12, October 28, 1969. Second Moon Mission.

ATLAS How would you like the job of standing up on your two feet and supporting all of space? Not so good? In Greek mythology, ATLAS had to hold up the heavens on his shoulders. Today ATLAS is the name for a series of liquid-fueled boosters. On December 18, 1958, an ATLAS launched *Project Score* into orbit from Cape Canaveral. It carried a tape recording of President Eisenhower's electronic message, "Merry Christmas." It made 500 orbits before re-entering the atmosphere and burning up on January 21, 1959.

The ATLAS booster was also used for the Mercury program. It's still used to put military satellites into orbit. The most famous flights were ATLAS Agenda D and ATLAS Centaur, the boosters for the Surveyor Moon Probes which soft-landed on the Moon, hopped about, and took thousands of images of the Moon's surface. These Moon probes helped in planning the Apollo program. See *Apollo, Booster, Images, Re-entry*.

An **ATMOSPHERE** is a body of gases surrounding a star, planet, or natural satellite. (Only two natural satellites in the solar system are thought to have atmospheres. They are Titan, a satellite of Jupiter, and Triton, a satellite of Uranus.) The Earth's ATMOSPHERE contains oxygen, nitrogen, and other gases which we need to live. The higher up you go the less ATMOSPHERE there is, so it is harder for you to breathe. There is no ATMOSPHERE like ours in space. See *Oxygen, Satellite, Space*.

ATTITUDE is the pitch, roll, and yaw of a rocket or satellite as it moves along its trajectory. See *Pitch, Roll, Trajectory, Yaw*.

An **AXIS** is an imaginary line that goes through the center of a planet perpendicular (up and down) to the equator. We say the Earth rotates about its AXIS. See *Equator, Revolution*.

B

BANDWIDTH is the number of radio frequencies needed to transmit data on a modulated radio wave. The more a radio wave is modulated, the more BANDWIDTH is needed for the radio wave, but the more BANDWIDTH there is, the more information can be sent on the radio wave. See *Modulation, Wave.*

BANDWIDTH COMPRESSION describes the reduction of BANDWIDTH needed to send data. When a satellite transmits pictures, it requires a lot of data or BANDWIDTH. Scientists have figured out ways to reduce, or compress, the amount of BANDWIDTH needed by satellites to send data back and forth. See *Bandwidth, Data, Imaging Equipment.*

BETA CLOTH Astronauts' space suits are made of BETA CLOTH, which is a soft fabric made of glass filament and other materials. Communications satellites launched by Space Shuttle Columbia were encased, or packaged, in individual sunshield compartments made of BETA CLOTH. Heating wires, like those in an electric blanket, run throughout the BETA CLOTH to keep the inside of the satellite at the right temperature. See *Temperature.*

The **BOOSTER** is usually the first or primary stage of a space craft which propels, or pushes, it into space. BOOSTERS are rocket stages that give the thrust needed to lift a spacecraft off the launching pad and into space. Secondary and other BOOSTERS also provide for extra thrust to change direction in later phases of a space vehicle's flight path. See *Atlas, Launching Pad, Propel, Rocket, Thrust.*

BURNOUT or **CUTOFF VELOCITY** is the speed reached when the propellant in the rocket is used up or cut off. See *Propellants.*

C

CARRIER WAVE is a simple, continuous radio wave. The amplitude and frequency of the carrier wave stay the same everywhere. A CARRIER WAVE is used to send information to and from a satellite. See *Amplitude, Frequency, Modulation, Radio Waves.*

CISLUNAR SPACE is the space between the Earth and the orbit of the Moon.

CIRCULAR ORBIT VELOCITY is the speed at which a satellite will orbit forever in a circle around a planet.

COLUMBIA was the first American space shuttle system to leave the Earth's atmosphere, re-enter the atmosphere, and land on Earth like an airplane. Its first voyage was April 12, 1981. On its first operational flight, November 11, 1982, COLUMBIA carried two communication satellites on board. At an altitude of 160 miles, the satellites were ejected from COLUMBIA and launched into orbit. See *Atmosphere, Communication Satellites, Orbit.*

COMMUNICATION SATELLITES make it possible for us to see news events on television as they happen in other parts of the world. If you get a phone call from your Aunt Mabel who's traveling all around the globe, the two of you are linked by a COMMUNICATION SATELLITE.

The experimental COMMUNICATION SATELLITES, SCORE, ECHO, TELSTAR, RELAY, and SYNCOM, were launched by the U.S.A. between 1958 and 1963. A satellite system called INTELSAT now spans the world, and domestic satellites serve individual countries. "It's a Small, Small World" is even truer now because COMMUNICATION SATELLITES keep the whole world in constant touch. See *Echo, Telstar 1.*

Space Shuttle, COLUMBIA, May 1, 1979.

Apollo 14 lunar module (landing craft). Brilliant sun reflected off the module, made the flare of light.

A **COMPONENT** is one part of the hardware used to make up a satellite system. COMPONENTS are used like building blocks to make a satellite. Ground stations are made up of similar COMPONENTS, but the satellite's are smaller, lighter, and more durable. They are listed below.

Satellite *solar cells* are COMPONENTS for electrical power. Satellites also have other COMPONENTS: *rockets* and *steering thrusters* for propulsion; *mechanical devices* such as cameras, radios, computers; *measurement equipment;* and *antennas* to transmit and receive data.

No **COMPUTERS,** no go! COMPUTERS are used to control the flight of space vehicles. There are so many things going on and the satellite moves so fast that no human could calculate and respond fast enough to do

the job. COMPUTERS are used to plan launches, flight paths, and orbital paths, send and receive data to and from satellites, and to process the data. People could not be in space without COMPUTERS. Analog and digital COMPUTERS are both used to fly spacecraft. The analog COMPUTER tells the digital COMPUTER the information it needs about thrust and attitude. Then the digital COMPUTER flies the ship based on the analog COMPUTER's information. See *Analog Computer, Attitude, Digital Computer.*

COSMIC RAYS are extremely high-energy atomic particles. They constantly bombard the Earth's upper atmosphere which keeps most of the rays from reaching the Earth's surface. See *Atmosphere.*

CUTOFF VELOCITY See *Burnout.*

ST. MARY SCHOOL
LIBRARY

D

DATA is the plural of *datum*, but most people say, "Data is . . ." A DATUM is a piece of raw information. Raw information could be a string of numbers that doesn't seem to mean very much. But after processing (usually by a digital computer), the meaning of the numbers becomes clear and we can then understand the information. Computers on satellites collect DATA. For example, a satellite notes the temperature of a planet's surface. This DATA, in a number code, is then sent to Earth by a radio transmitter. A ground station antenna catches the signal which is then made stronger and recorded on magnetic tape. It is fed to a computer which analyzes and processes the raw DATA into usable information. This information is printed or stored for people's immediate or future use. See *Antennas, Component, Transmit*. See also *Data* in the book *Computer TECH TALK*.

DECELERATION is slowing down. If you and your bike are about to run into a tree, it's time for some DECELERATION. Use the brakes. If a satellite DECELERATES enough to lose its orbital velocity, it's pulled back to Earth. If it doesn't burn up in the atmosphere, it crashes onto the Earth. See *Orbital Velocity*.

The **DIGITAL COMPUTER** works with numbers, whereas an analog computer works with natural changes such as temperature or speed. A DIGITAL COMPUTER reads in number data and processes it into information. This COMPUTER works only with numbers and types out the answers as numbers. A DIGITAL COMPUTER has components such as a CPU (central processing unit), CRT (cathode ray tube like the picture tube on a television), and a keyboard. See *Analog Computers, Component* and the book *Computer TECH TALK*.

E

An **ECHO** is sound bouncing back from the wall of a big room or a canyon. The ECHO satellite was the first communication satellite placed in a 1,000-mile orbit by NASA on August 12, 1960. It was a 135-foot silvery balloon which reflected radio signals from the Earth off its surface and back to Earth. This kind of satellite is called passive because it only reflects signals and does no work. The Echo could be seen for many years as it orbited the Earth. See *Communication Satellites, NASA, Passive Satellite.*

ELLIPSE, ELLIPTICAL An ELLIPSE is a flattened circle. When a satellite goes around the Earth, its orbit is not a perfect circle but an ELLIPSE. This is called an ELLIPTICAL orbit. Sometimes the satellite is very close to Earth (perigee) and at other times it's very distant (apogee). See *Apogee, Orbit, Perigee.*

ENCODING is the way information is put on a modulated radio wave in order to send information from a satellite to Earth. See *Modulation, Radio Waves.*

An **ENCOUNTER** is a meeting, so that's the term used by space scientists to describe the time when a spacecraft gets close enough to "meet" a planet. Voyagers 1 and 2 ENCOUNTERED Jupiter and Saturn and other planets. These probes sent back very clear images of Jupiter and Saturn, their rings, and moons (or satellites). See *Imaging Equipment, Moons, Planet, Probe, Voyager.*

This calls for some DECELERATION!

The **EQUATOR** is an imaginary line drawn around the center of the Earth exactly halfway between the North and South Poles. The EQUATOR divides the northern half of the globe, or hemisphere, from the southern hemisphere of the Earth. The EQUATOR and other imaginary lines on the globe map of the Earth were made up by early map makers to help people locate specific places on the Earth.

EROSION GAUGES are strips of metal attached to the outside of a satellite. They measure the size of meteors that strike a spacecraft. As these tiny particles of rock smash into a satellite, they wear away the EROSION GAUGES. Fastened to the EROSION GAUGES are wires that carry information about the EROSION to a radio inside the satellite. The radio sends the information back to Earth. See *Antennas, Meteor.*

ESCAPE VELOCITY is the speed at which a rocket must travel straight up to escape the gravity of the body from which it is launched. From Earth, the ESCAPE VELOCITY is seven miles per second. From Jupiter, the ESCAPE VELOCITY is 36.7 miles per second.

EXPLORER I was the third satellite ever launched into outer space. It was cylinder-shaped, eighty inches long, six inches wide, and weighed 31 pounds. It was launched January 31, 1958 by the United States. On May 23, 1958, its batteries stopped working, but it did not re-enter the Earth's atmosphere until March 31, 1970. If you wonder why, read about *Deceleration, Gravity, Inertia, and Orbital Velocity.*

EXTRAPLANETARY SPACE is the space beyond a particular planet's orbit. See *Space.*

EXTRATERRESTRIAL SPACE is the space outside of the Earth's atmosphere. See *Space.*

Dr. W. H. Pickering, Dr. James A. van Allen, and Dr. Wernher von Braun hold the EXPLORER 1, launched January 31, 1958.

F

FREQUENCY is one of the characteristics of a wave. All waves go through cycles. FREQUENCY is the number of cycles per second of a wave. See *Wave*.

FUEL is any energy-yielding material used to drive a vehicle. The cereal you had for breakfast is the FUEL that gives you the energy to pedal your bike to school. FUELS may be liquids, such as gasoline or kerosene. Other FUELS can be powders that burn rapidly or solid chunks that burn a long time. See *Hydrazine, Hydrogen Peroxide, Kerosene, Propellants*.

G

You live in a **GALAXY,** but then of course you also live in a solar system, and on a planet. A GALAXY is a huge group of stars held together by gravitation and separated from other GALAXIES. So far, we have used satellites to explore only our solar system, but some will continue to move out into our GALAXY, called the Milky Way. See *Gravity, Planet, Pioneer, Voyager*.

GAMMA RAYS are rays of high energy that come in very short wave-lengths. They are produced by nuclear reactions including those originating in the Sun.

A **GEODETIC SATELLITE** is one designed to map the Earth. It does this in many ways. What's so special about it is that it's way out there in space making more accurate maps than people have ever been able to make.

GEMINI comes from the Latin word for twin, *geminus.* In *Satellite TECH TALK,* GEMINI was an early space project that sent two-man capsules into space. GEMINI astronauts learned how to join two space ships together while they orbited the Earth. This project included eight flights that were important steps to be taken before we could send people to the Moon. The GEMINI flights showed us some of the effects of space travel on humans. See *Mercury, Apollo.*

A **GEOSYNCHRONOUS** satellite is one that's 22,300 miles above the Earth. It takes 24 hours for it to orbit the Earth. That means it is over the same spot on the Earth at all times. Looking at it from the Earth, it would appear to be stationary (never moving).

Robert H. **GODDARD** was called a dreamer and "Moon man" for a long time while he experimented with liquid-fuel rockets. One of his tests proved that a rocket could work in a vacuum, or where there is no air. People stopped laughing at Mr. GODDARD in 1935, when he fired the first rocket to go faster than the speed of sound. The GODDARD Space Flight Center is named in his honor. See *Von Braun, Wernher.*

GRAVITY is a force that attracts bodies toward each other. GRAVITY exists everywhere in the universe. The attraction between the Earth and the Moon is an example of GRAVITY.

GRAVITY is both good and bad for satellites. Were it not for GRAVITY, a satellite would never orbit the Earth. The satellite would just fly off into space. But it's also GRAVITY that pulls a satellite out of orbit and back to Earth. See *Orbit, Universe.*

GRAVITY BOOST Satellites and spacecraft can use a planet's GRAVITY to BOOST their speed. As the satellite in orbit gets closer to the planet, it picks up a great deal of speed because the pull of GRAVITY increases. A satellite goes fastest at its perigee and slowest at its apogee. See *Apogee, Perigee.*

GROUND STATION See *Component.*

A **GYROSCOPE** is a fast-spinning object that tries to keep its position on an axis. A top is a good example of a GYROSCOPE in action. See *Axis, Inertia, Inertial Guidance.*

H

The **HELIOPAUSE** is the farthest reach of our Sun's magnetic field. See *Magnetic Field*.

HYDRAZINE is one of several very powerful liquid fuels used to propel rockets. See *Fuel, Propellants*.

HYDROGEN PEROXIDE, in its pure state, burns as a fuel for rockets. It must be handled very carefully because it blows up easily. Don't worry, the HYDROGEN PEROXIDE in the bottle under your bathroom sink is mostly water.

At the GODDARD Space Flight Center, technicians prepare the Dynamics Explorer-B spacecraft for testing. Instruments will explore Earth's magnetosphere, ionosphere, and plasmasphere.

A **HYPERBOLIC ORBIT** is not really an orbit, but a trajectory. The satellite goes by the planet only once, shoots into space, and never returns to that planet again. It goes even faster than a satellite in a *parabolic orbit*. Pioneer 10, launched in 1972, has done a series of HYPERBOLIC ORBITS with Mars, Jupiter, Saturn, Uranus, Neptune, and Pluto. It sent back pictures never before seen by Earth people. When Pioneer 10 orbited Pluto, which is three billion miles away, its radio signals took 4 hours and 15 minutes to reach Earth. That's because radio signals travel at the speed of light and that's how long it takes light to travel three billion miles. Now that's far, far away. See *Parabolic Orbit, Trajectory.*

I

IMAGES are what we call the pictures taken by a satellite. IMAGES are not true photographs, but electronic pictures created in much the same way that a television camera does. See *Imaging Equipment.*

IMAGING EQUIPMENT is used on space flights to take pictures that will be sent back to Earth. It works like a television camera rather than like a camera that uses film which must be developed. On unmanned space flights, an electronic camera can be remotely controlled by radio. See *Radio Control, Remote Control.*

INERTIA is the property of matter that makes it obey one of the laws of motion that says, "A body in motion tends to remain in motion; a body at rest tends to remain at rest unless acted upon by an outside force." To overcome INERTIA, whether to move a body at rest or to stop a body in motion, takes energy.

If your dog is enjoying the INERTIA of a body at rest, the energy of a cat in motion could put your dog in motion.

INERTIAL GUIDANCE is a way of steering a satellite by sensing its motion about a stable object like a gyroscope that the satellite carries along with it. A gyroscope tends to stay in a fixed position, and the satellite steers itself by sensing the positions of its gyroscopes. Actually, every time the gyroscopes change, the analog computer tells the digital computer, which in turn flies the ship on a correct course. See *Analog Computer, Computers, Digital Computer, Gyroscope.*

IMAGING EQUIPMENT, built for Voyager spacecraft, takes pictures of planets, moons, and asteroids to be sent back to Earth.

I/O DEVICE or **INPUT/OUT-PUT DEVICE** might be a television or a printer. Its INPUT job is to receive data from the satellite and convert it into a format a computer can use which in turn processes the data. Its OUTPUT job is to present the processed data in a form people can easily understand. It's like changing 1980s teen slang into adult language so grown-ups could understand what the teens were saying. (I/O DEVICES are "radical" but never "grody to the max!")

INTERGALACTIC SPACE is the space between galaxies. See *Galaxy, Space.*

INTERPLANETARY SPACE is the space within the solar system. See *Solar System, Space.*

INTERSTELLAR SPACE is the space between stars within a galaxy. See *Galaxy, Space.*

INERTIA

MOTION

J

JPL, or **J**et **P**ropulsion Laboratory, is part of the California Institute of Technology. JPL works for NASA to develop space exploration projects.

K

KEROSENE is a fast-burning fuel that gives off heat and energy as it burns. Rocket engines sometimes use KEROSENE for fuel. See *Rocket Engine.*

Experiment #421
To prove this umbrella will give me a soft LANDING.

L

LAND AND SEA OBSERVATION SATELLITES use microwave, x-ray, and infrared wavelengths to obtain valuable data about land and sea resources. Called LANDSAT, this series, launched in 1978, made estimates of world wheat production, mineral and oil supplies, and geologic maps. They grouped and counted major crops in special areas of the U.S.A., as well as lakes, rivers, reservoirs, and ponds for dam-safety studies and water-resource planning. They can do these wonderful things because their sensors can tell the difference between land and sea, cities and fields, corn and wheat. They can even tell the difference between healthy and diseased crops. LANDSAT can measure ocean currents, tides, rain rate, and the age, depth, size, and motion of sea ice. We are constantly learning new things about our world because of satellites. See *Microwaves.*

LANDING, soft or hard? You've made both after a jump or a fall. If, after flight, a vehicle makes a hard LANDING, there's nothing to do but pick up the pieces. After a soft LANDING, a vehicle may be in good enough condition to fly again or to walk away from. On September 12, 1959, the USSR probe, Luna 2, was the first one to impact the Moon (make a hard LANDING). On January 31, 1966, the USSR probe, Luna 9, was the first man-made object to soft LAND on the Moon and to transmit pictures of the Moon's surface.

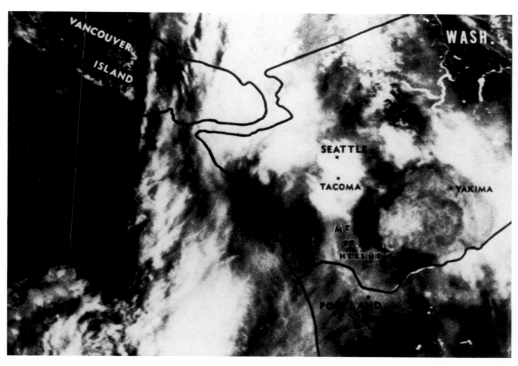

Mt. St. Helens hides under its cloud of ash and steam in this image taken by a weather satellite, May 18, 1980. Similar images are taken by LAND AND SEA OBSERVATION SATELLITES.

Some of the **LAUNCH SITES** in the USA include Cape Canaveral or Kennedy in Florida and Vandenberg Air Force Base in California. Such bases handle all the details for the LAUNCHING of space vehicles. Not only have these LAUNCH SITES boosted satellites, they've boosted the economies of the surrounding areas. Just think how many hotdogs you could sell to all the reporters and spectators who come to witness a LAUNCHING.

A **LAUNCHING PAD** is a structure from which a rocket can be fired safely and accurately.

LIFTOFF! That's what all rocket people like to see. It's the moment the rocket moves up, off the launching pad. It often means a satellite is on its way to be put into orbit. See *Launching Pad, Orbit, Rocket.*

LUNA 1 was sent up by the Soviet Union as a Moon probe. It went past the Moon and is now traveling around the Sun.

M

A **MAGNETIC FIELD** is the region around an object where the pull on a piece of iron can be felt or measured. We say the object has a MAGNETIC FIELD or is simply MAGNETIC. Many bodies in space have MAGNETIC FIELDS. Earth does, but the Moon does not.

A **MAGNETOMETER** measures the strength of a magnetic field.

Satellites often carry MAGNETOMETERS to measure the magnetic fields of planets. This helps scientists know what the planets and other bodies are made of. See *Magnetic Field.*

MAGNETOSPHERE is the space around a body that includes its magnetic field. See *Magnetic Field.*

LIFTOFF! Voyager 2, August 20, 1977, (left) and liftoff of the Viking mission in 1975, (bottom).

MARINER was a probe program (1962-69). It included six probes. MARINERS 1, 2, 3, and 5 flew by Venus. MARINERS 4, 5, and 7 flew by Mars. From these probes, scientists learned that Venus has a high surface temperature and no magnetic field or radiation belt. They also learned that about 45 miles above this planet's surface is a cloud cover about 15 miles thick. The Mars flybys told us a lot about the pitted surface, thin atmosphere, and temperatures on that planet. The MARINER program gave us valuable scientific information, but no Martians were sighted. See *Magnetic Field, Probe, Radiation Belts.*

MATTER is anything that has mass and takes up space. There is a theory that billions of years ago all MATTER was one huge mass that exploded. This is the Big Bang theory of how our universe began. See *Universe.*

The **MERCURY** missions were the first phase of the Apollo program. They were manned spacecraft, each containing one astronaut. Alan Shepard was the first American sent into space in 1961. John Glenn first orbited the Earth in 1962. All six MERCURY flights taught people some of what they needed to know to conquer space. See *Apollo, Gemini.*

MARINER 10, launched in November, 1973 flew by Venus and encountered Mercury three times.

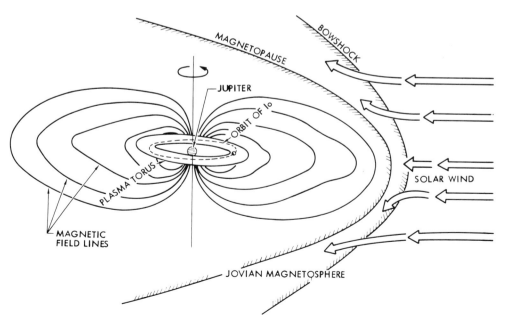

CROSS SECTION OF JOVIAN MAGNETOSPHERE

A **METEOR** is a space rock that falls to Earth at high speeds. As it falls, it burns up. The result is a streak of light in the sky that people call a "shooting star." See *Meteorite.*

METEOR BUMPERS are used to protect space vehicles from damage caused by bumping into meteors. They are thin shields around the vehicle that weaken the impact energy of a meteor's particles. They protect the vehicle the way bumpers protect the body of a car. See *Meteor.*

A **METEORITE** is the unburned part of a meteor that lands on the Earth. See *Meteor.*

MICROMETEORS are microscopic meteorites. Called space dust, they are plentiful in space. After a vehicle flies through a bunch of MICROMETEORS, it looks as though it has been sandblasted.

MICROWAVES are short wavelength, high frequency, electrical waves. Since MICROWAVES tend to travel in very straight lines, they can be beamed long distances between satellites or between satellites and ground stations. Without MICROWAVES, it would be impossible to communicate with satellites. See *Ground Station, Radar.*

MIDAS It's Monday morning and *everything* you touch turns to gold. A Greek myth tells of a king named MIDAS who was given the power to turn everything he touched into gold. In the 1960s, MIDAS (**MI**ssile **D**efense **A**larm **S**ystem) was an American reconnaissance satellite program. The satellites used infrared scanners to detect enemy Intercontinental Ballistic Missiles in early stages of flight. See *Reconnaissance Satellites.*

MISSION CONTROL All U.S. manned space missions are controlled from MISSION CONTROL in Houston, Texas. While flight paths are calculated at MISSION CONTROL, the space vehicle is usually launched from Cape Canaveral in Florida. MISSION CONTROL keeps in constant touch with the space vehicle and the astronauts can "phone home."

MILKY WAY is the name of the galaxy we live in. No one really knows how many stars are in the MILKY WAY, but according to Larousse's *Guide to the Stars*, there are 100 billion. Our Sun is one of those stars located near the edge of the galaxy. See *Galaxy*.

MODULATION changes *one* of the characteristics of a radio frequency carrier wave. Scientists use the changes in the wave to transfer data to and from a satellite. If the MODULATION changes the amplitude, it's called amplitude MODULATION or AM. This is the same MODULATION used by your AM radio station. If the wave characteristic changed is the frequency, it is abbreviated FM. Again, this is the MODULATION your FM radio station uses. See *Amplitude, Frequency, Carrier Wave, Radio Waves, Wave*. See the book *Radio TECH TALK*.

MOONS Moons are natural satellites. We have one pretty good MOON orbiting Earth. Some other planets have many MOONS or natural satellites. Still others have none. The Voyager Missions discovered two new MOONS of Jupiter that had not been known before. Voyagers 1 and 2 showed that Jupiter has 16 MOONS and Saturn has 21 MOONS. See *Encounter, Satellite, Voyager.*

Image of one of Jupiter's MOONS, Io, made March 4, 1979 by equipment aboard Voyager 1 about 500,000 miles from Io.

N

NADIR is an imaginary line pointing from a satellite straight through the center of the planet it is orbiting.

NASA is the **N**ational **A**eronautics and **S**pace **A**dministration. That's a big name for an important part of the U.S. government. NASA is important because it takes charge of all U.S. activities in space.

NAVIGATION SATELLITES use radio signals to pinpoint exact locations on Earth. The U.S. TRANSIT system of NAVIGATION SATELLITES works all around the world, mostly for ships. NAVSTAR is a more advanced system of 24 satellites. They are positioned in three rings of eight satellites each at an altitude of 20,000 miles. Columbus never would have mixed up India and the Western Hemisphere if he'd been able to use a NAVIGATION SATELLITE. Does this mean America wouldn't exist if Columbus had not discovered it?

O

OAO, the **O**rbiting **A**stronomical **O**bservatory was the NASA probe program used for astronomical studies of the planets and other bodies in space, otherwise known as *celestial bodies.*

OGO, Orbiting **G**eophysical **O**bservatory was a NASA probe program with six satellites launched between 1964 and 1969. The satellites carried equipment for geophysical experiments which studied the effects on the Earth of motion, matter, and energy from within the planet and from outer space.

An **ORBIT** is a path around an object. The Earth and all the other planets follow their ORBITS around the Sun. It takes the Earth 365¼ days to ORBIT the Sun. The Moon ORBITS the Earth. Most ORBITS are elliptical in shape. John Glenn was the first American to go into an Earth ORBIT on February 20, 1962. See *Apogee, Ellipse, Elliptical, Perigee.*

ORBITAL means having to do with an orbit. See *Orbit.*

ORBITAL PERIOD is the length of time it takes one body to make a complete orbit around another body.

ORBITAL VELOCITY is the speed at which any spacecraft must move in order not to fall onto the body (planet or star) it is orbiting. See *Orbit, Planet.*

OSO, Orbiting **S**olar **O**bservatory helps us study the Sun. With it, scientists discovered solar wind, a constant flow of low-energy particles streaming out from the Sun. These particles can whip into storms with winds as fast as 1000 miles per second. Such storms cause disturbances in the Earth's

NOVA, the advanced Navy navigation satellite with station-keeping propulsion system. See Propulsion System, Station Keeping.

magnetic field and produce the aurora borealis, or northern lights often seen in Alaska and other northern regions. Now we know that Mr. Sun can blow as well as burn. See *Magnetic Field.*

An **OXIDIZER** is a chemical that burns the fuel during combustion in a rocket. Outside the Earth's atmosphere, there is no OXIDIZER to burn the fuel, so a rocket must carry its own OXIDIZER for the combustion of fuel. See *Atmosphere, Fuel, Oxygen.*

OXYGEN is a basic element present in the Earth's atmosphere. Fuels burn in the presence of OXYGEN. See *Atmosphere, Fuel, Oxidizer, Propellants.*

P

A **PARABOLIC ORBIT** is the orbit that separates elliptical and hyperbolic orbits. If a satellite in an elliptical orbit is speeded up, there comes a point at which the satellite has just enough speed so that it can no longer be held by a planet's gravitational field and the satellite leaves the planet. It goes into PARABOLIC ORBIT, which is actually a trajectory. The satellite only passes by the planet once and leaves, never to return to that planet again. See *Ellipse, Elliptical, Hyperbolic Orbit, Trajectory.*

A **PASSIVE SATELLITE** does not receive or transmit signals. It may be one like the ECHO Satellite which has no working parts. See *Active Satellite, Echo.*

A **PAYLOAD** is anything a missile or rocket ship carries. A satellite is sometimes the PAYLOAD of a rocket. See *Rocket, Satellite.*

PERIGEE is the point in an orbit closest to the body being circled. Earth is at the PERIGEE of its orbit when it's closest to the Sun. A satellite in an elliptical orbit around our planet is at PERIGEE when it's closest to the Earth. See *Apogee, Ellipse, Elliptical, Orbit, Planet.*

A **PERTURBATION** is a small change or defect in a regular pattern. The result of PERTURBATIONS keep a satellite's orbit from staying always the same in size, shape, and direction. The gravitational attraction at the bulge in the Earth's equator, the drag of the atmosphere, and the pull of the Sun and the Moon may affect a satellite's orbit.

If you were to run in a circle, or in an orbit, around a tree, but couldn't make your circle quite perfect because of a rock or hole in the ground, your running circle would have PERTURBATIONS.

PITCH is the angle a rocket leans as it takes off into space. It changes the trajectory of the rocket. See *Attitude, Roll, Trajectory, Yaw.*

PIONEER The brave people who rode their covered wagons out to settle the western United States were PIONEERS. In *Satellite Tech Talk,* PIONEER is a series of probes sent to explore space—the Earth's last frontier. PIONEERS 1, 2, and 3, launched a month apart in late 1958, all had failures in propulsion. PIONEER 10, sent to the Moon, missed it by some 37,300 miles, and plunged into solar orbit. (Oh, well, some California-bound PIONEERS never made it past the Mississippi River.) PIONEER 10, launched in 1972, has continued to send back pictures. It left the solar system in 1983. Scientists expect it to get close to the nearest star in 10,000 years. See *Propulsion System.*

PERTURBATION?

A **PLANET** is a large body that revolves around a star. The Earth is one of nine known PLANETS that orbit around our star, the Sun. Some brief facts about the PLANETS and probes of them are shown below.

A good way to remember the PLANETS in order from closest to the Sun to the farthest is the sentence, "**M**ary **V**isits **E**very **M**onday **A**nd **J**ust **S**tays **U**ntil **N**oon, **P**eriod." The first letter of each word in this sentence represents the initial of each PLANET in order going out from the Sun. The "a" in "and" stands for the asteroids orbiting between the orbits of Mars and Jupiter. Sometimes the orbit of Pluto takes it within the orbit of Neptune, and for a few years it is *not* the farthest PLANET from the Sun. During that time you say, ". . . **A**nd **S**tays **U**ntil **P**ractically **N**oon."

POGO, Polar **O**rbiting **G**eophysical **O**bservatory probes the same way OGO does but it's in an orbit that circles over the north and south poles. See *OGO, Probe*.

PLANET	DIAMETER (in miles)	ORBITAL PERIOD	SATELLITE ENCOUNTERS
Mercury	3,000	88 days	none
Venus	7,600	225 days	Mariner, Venera (USSR)
Earth	7,900	365¼ days	
Mars	4,200	687 days	Mariner, Pioneer, Viking
Jupiter	87,000	12 years	Pioneer, Voyager
Saturn	71,500	29½ years	Pioneer, Voyager
Uranus	29,500	84 years	Pioneer, Voyager in 1986
Neptune	26,800	165 years	Pioneer, Voyager in 1989
Pluto	3,600	248 years	Pioneer

Earth, a solid PLANET, and Jupiter, a gaseous PLANET, compared in size.

PROBE Have you ever seen someone PROBE the breakfast cereal? That person was ·exploring to see if there were any raisins. In *Satellite Tech Talk* PROBES are craft that escape the Earth's gravitational field and travel through cislunar or interplanetary space to explore. The difference between the interplanetary PROBE and a satellite orbiting the Earth is one of mission, or purpose, rather than how it's made. PROBES have to be more powerful, travel farther, and last longer. Each PROBE has a target planet to investigate with imaging

equipment and measuring devices. Some make soft landings, some hard land, but most just fly by or make an encounter. See *Cislunar Space, Encounter, Imaging Equipment, Interplanetary Space, Mariner, Pioneer, Viking, Voyager.*

PROGRAMS are used for a satellite to plan and execute its launch and journey into space. These PROGRAMS are a set of instructions the computer uses to direct the satellite in doing specific tasks such as measuring a magnetic field or the temperature of a planet's surface. See *Computers, Magnetic Field, Robot, Viking.*

You **PROPEL** yourself ahead when you ride your bicycle. The power and energy of your legs turning the pedals is your bicycle's propellant. Rockets and satellites are PROPELLED through space by rocket engines. See *Fuel, Propellants, Propulsion System, Rocket, Rocket Engine.*

THE GREAT RAISIN PROBE

PROPELLANTS come in liquid and solid forms or combinations of fuels. They are often mixed with oxidizers which cause them to burn and develop thrust to lift or propel a rocket or satellite. See *Fuel, Oxidizer, Thrust.*

A **PROPULSION SYSTEM** is the equipment that makes something move. If you throw a ball, you provide the ball's PROPULSION SYSTEM. For rockets and satellites, the power from burning fuel provides the PROPULSION. See *Fuel, Propellants.*

R

The word "**RADAR**" stands for **Ra**dio **D**etecting **A**nd **R**anging. It's a radio system used to locate an object such as a cloud, airplane, or spacecraft. RADAR can also measure size and speed of these as well as of a car moving toward or away from a RADAR-equipped police or sheriff's car.

RADIATION is the letting out of energy. It can be in the form of particles, light, or different kinds of waves. We have to be careful not to be exposed to too much RADIATION because it has a harmful effect on our bodies.

The Earth's atmosphere protects us from most of the RADIATION found in space. People who travel in space need special equipment to protect them from it. See *Atmosphere.*

RADIATION BELTS are zones of high-energy radiation around a planet or star. See *Van Allen Belts.*

You have **RADIO CONTROL** when you guide and direct an object by transmitting radio commands to its receiver. Radio commands can travel great distances and give very complex instructions. People use RADIO CONTROL to tell a satellite hundreds of thousands of miles from the Earth what jobs to perform. See *Receiver, Transmit.*

RADIO WAVES are electrical energy that can carry information. The information in the RADIO WAVE could be a sound, music, numbers, or pictures as on television. See *Imaging Equipment, Wave.*

RANGER If you wore a black mask and rode a white horse,

you could be called the Lone RANGER. But when you talk about satellites and space, the name RANGER means something else. The RANGER probes (1961-63) were sent to the Moon to provide data to help plan a landing craft for the

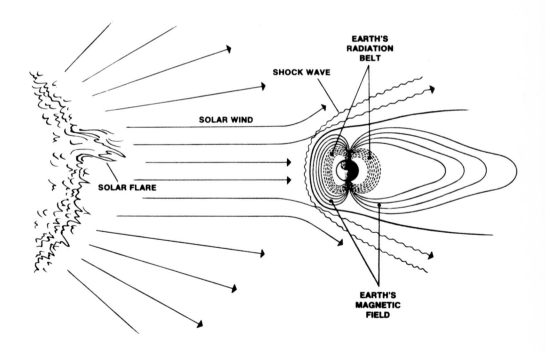

Solar winds affect Earth's RADIATION BELTS, often causing northern lights and magnetic storms that disrupt radio communications. Dynamics Explorer satellites investigate such happenings. See photos, page 22, 48.

manned Apollo program. The nine RANGER probes returned 12,954 pictures of the Moon's surface. See *Imaging Equipment, Probe.*

RECEIVER The small radio you carry around is a radio RECEIVER. The RECEIVER in a satellite changes radio signals into information for the spacecraft. The signals a satellite *receives* tell it what to do. See *Transmit.*

RECONNAISSANCE SATELLITES are used to take pictures of a planet's surface. COSMOS and SAMOS are two satellite systems launched by the USSR and USA respectively. These RECONNAISSANCE SATELLITES fly over other countries and take pictures of what's going on.

RE-ENTRY If your class comes in from recess and makes too much noise, your teacher may tell you to go outside and make a classroom RE-ENTRY. Satellites don't come in from recess

but they sometimes make a RE-ENTRY into the Earth's atmosphere after being in orbit. Are you ever in orbit at recess? See *Atmosphere, Orbit.*

REMOTE CONTROL is the directing of a machine from some distance. It's usually done by radio REMOTE CONTROL. See *Radio Control.*

REVOLUTION is the spinning of an object, such as the Earth which makes one REVOLUTION about its axis every 24 hours. See *Axis.*

The Earth **REVOLVES** around the Sun once every year as it makes 365¼ revolutions about its axis. See *Axis, Orbit, Revolution.*

A **ROBOT** is a machine operated by a computer. Some satellites are ROBOTS when some or all of their jobs are programmed on a computer. See *Computers, Programs, Surveyor, Viking, Voyager.*

*A true photograph of Astronaut E. E. (Buzz) Aldrin
and the Moon's surface.*

A **ROCKET** is the only type of vehicle that works in space. Outside the earth's atmosphere there is no oxygen which is needed to burn fuel, so ROCKET engines, fueled by propellants with oxidizers, are needed for space travel. ROCK-ETS are used to lift satellites into space. Once the ROCKET reaches outer space, the sat-

ellite is released and the ROCKET, or booster, falls away. Sometimes small ROCKET engines are part of a satellite. They're used to change the flight path from time to time. See *Rocket Engine, Radio Control, Oxidizer, Oxygen, Space.*

A **ROCKET ENGINE** works because of a simple law of motion. "For every action, there is an equal and opposite reaction." When you let go of an inflated balloon, the air rushing out the hole causes the balloon to go in the opposite direction. The balloon is a simple ROCKET ENGINE powered by air pressure. In a rocket, the engine combines fuel and oxidizer to create a jet of hot gases. The force of heated air and gases leaving the back of the engine causes the craft to move forward. See *Fuel.*

ROLL is the spin of a rocket. It does not change the trajectory or the course of the rocket. See *Attitude, Pitch, Spin Stabilization, Yaw.*

Powerful ROCKET ENGINES launch Columbia, a spacecraft designed to launch satellites. Columbia itself has additional ROCKET ENGINES to keep it on course.

S

SAFE AND ARM DEVICE People who shoot pistols in target practice know what SAFE AND ARM DEVICES do. Here's how they work. If you cock a pistol, it's armed, ready to shoot instantly. But if you put on the safety catch, the pistol is still armed but *safe*. You can't fire until the safety catch is released.

A rocket can be armed, loaded with fuel, but a SAFE AND ARM DEVICE keeps the rocket from firing until the right time. See *Rocket*.

A **SATELLITE** is any object that moves in orbit around another object. Natural SATELLITES include the Earth's Moon and the many moons around other planets. Manmade or artificial SATELLITES were first orbited in 1957. See *Moons, Orbit, Sputnik I and II, Vanguard 1*.

A pair of earth-orbiting Dynamics Explorers study northern lights and radio disturbances.

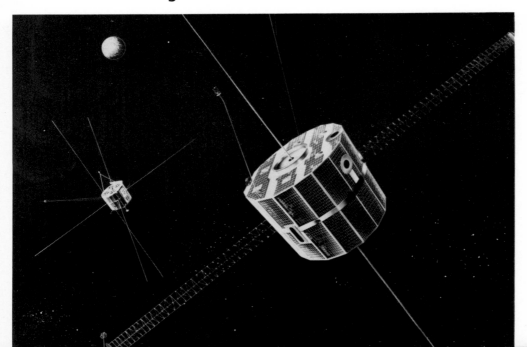

A **SATELLITE PERIOD**, also called an orbital period, is the time it takes a satellite to complete its orbit around a planet. See *Planet*.

SCIENTIFIC RESEARCH SATELLITES are used to study astronomical objects such as planets and stars or the space around the Earth. Explorer I was the first. See *OGO, OSO, POGO*.

SKYLAB was an American space station launched in May, 1973. It was placed in Earth orbit at an altitude of 271 miles. The crews of Apollo 18, 19, and 20 lived on it 28 days, 59 days, and 84 days respectively. In July, 1978, SKYLAB, with no crew on board, fell out of orbit. Its remains landed in Australia.

SOLAR means "of the Sun."

A **SOLAR CELL** is a flat disk that can produce electrical energy from sunlight. The disks are connected into large panels to provide space vehicles with electrical power.

SOLAR ENERGY is power derived from the Sun's ENERGY. Many satellites have electrical equipment on board. SOLAR batteries and other forms of SOLAR ENERGY are used to power this equipment.

A **SOLAR PANEL** is a group of solar cells connected to each other to produce a large amount of electrical energy. See *Solar Cell.*

The **SOLAR SYSTEM** is where you live. It includes the Sun, which is a star. The SOLAR SYSTEM also includes the planets, asteroids, and the Sun's magnetic field. That's a pretty huge place, but very, very small when you know the SOLAR SYSTEM is a speck on the edge of a galaxy that includes hundreds of billions of other stars. See *Asteroid, Galaxy, Magnetic Field, Milky Way, Planet.*

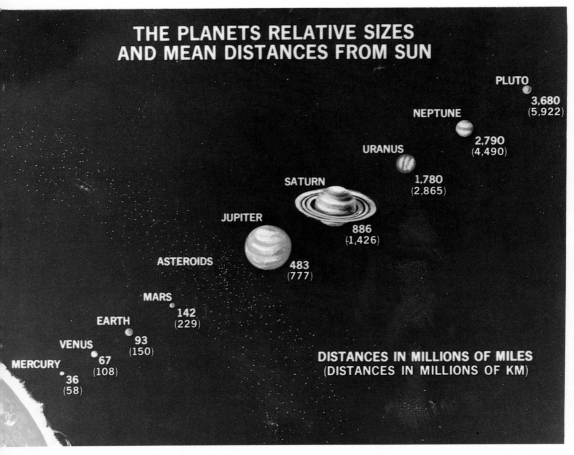

THE PLANETS RELATIVE SIZES AND MEAN DISTANCES FROM SUN

PLUTO
3,680
(5,922)

NEPTUNE
2,790
(4,490)

URANUS
1,780
(2,865)

SATURN
886
(1,426)

JUPITER
483
(777)

ASTEROIDS

MARS
142
(229)

EARTH
93
(150)

VENUS
67
(108)

MERCURY
36
(58)

DISTANCES IN MILLIONS OF MILES
(DISTANCES IN MILLIONS OF KM)

Where do you live in this SOLAR SYSTEM?

SPACE is the area outside the Earth's atmosphere. There is no air in SPACE that Earth people can breathe. *Extraplanetary* SPACE is the SPACE around any planet. *Extraterrestrial* SPACE is SPACE beyond the Earth. *Cislunar* or *interlunar* SPACE is between the Earth and the Moon. *Interplanetary* SPACE is the SPACE between planets. *Interstellar* SPACE is between stars in a galaxy. *Intergalactic* SPACE is that between the galaxies within the universe. SPACE outside the universe is not defined. Since many of the SPACE terms overlap, we'll just play it safe and call them *outer* SPACE. See *Galaxy, Universe.*

SPACE CENTERS are places where spacecraft may be built, launched, and/or monitored (watched and controlled). Sometimes astronauts are trained at SPACE CENTERS. Cape Canaveral, Mission Control in Houston, Texas, Kennedy SPACE CENTER, and Vandenburg Air Force Base are some of the SPACE CENTERS in the U.S.A.

SPACE DUST See *Micrometeors.*

SPACE PLATFORM You live on a SPACE PLATFORM called Earth. If you send a satellite into orbit and it becomes a place to launch another satellite, then you have launched a SPACE PLATFORM from which to launch a satellite.

SPACE SHUTTLE See *Columbia.*

A **SPACE STATION** is an orbiting space vehicle where people can live. SKYLAB (USA) and SALYUT (USSR) were the first SPACE STATIONS launched. See *Orbit, Skylab.*

SPIN STABILIZATION A good example of SPIN STABILIZATION is a carefully thrown forward pass of a football. The spinning helps keep the ball going in the right direction without tumbling. Some rockets have SPIN STABILIZATION to keep them stabilized and on course. See *Pitch, Yaw.*

SPUTNIK I was the first man-made satellite sent into outer space. It was launched by the Soviet Union on October 4, 1957. SPUTNIK I was 23 inches in diameter (the distance from one side of a circle through the center to the other side) and weighed 184 pounds. It had four antennas and orbited the Earth for three months. See *Antenna, Orbit.*

SPUTNIK II was sent into space by the Soviet Union on November 3, 1957. Cylinder-shaped, measuring 19 feet long and 4 feet wide, SPUTNIK II weighed 1,120 pounds. Aboard SPUTNIK II was the first live passenger, Laika the dog. SPUTNIK II stayed in orbit for six months, but Laika died after a few days in space.

STATION KEEPING is a process of using an on-board satellite propulsion system to keep a satellite in its correct orbit. STATION KEEPING thrusters correct forces, such as magnetic attractions to the Earth's poles and equators, on low-orbiting satellites. STATION KEEPING makes a high-orbiting satellite stay on the right path, even when it's attracted by forces of the Sun and the Moon. See *Perturbation, Propulsion System.*

SURVEYOR was a series of seven probes (1966-68) sent to soft-land on the Moon. They were to find the best spots for the Apollo crews to land. As space robots, these vehicles had soil scoops with which to pick up samples and bring them back to Earth to be studied. The SURVEYORS were the first earthlings to sample the Moon's surface. See *Apollo, Probe, Robot.*

Model of Surveyor 3 orbits a model of our Moon.

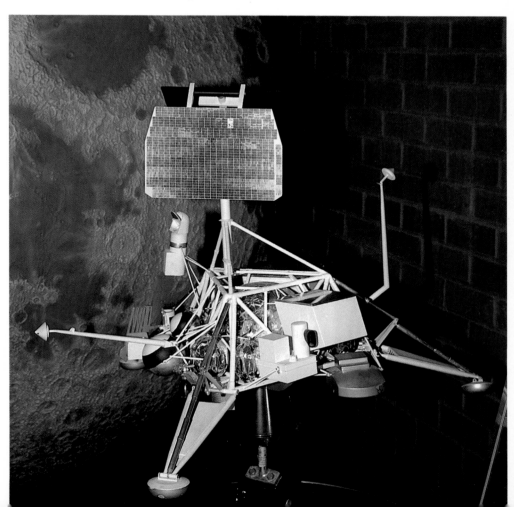

T

TELEMETRY is the process of gathering, coding, and transmitting data to Earth from a satellite. This is done with radio signals. See *Data, Transmit.*

TELSTAR 1 was the first satellite to receive and transmit almost all kinds of microwave communication. It was launched by American Telephone and Telegraph Company in 1962. It was destroyed by radiation in the Van Allen Belts. See *Microwaves, Receiver, Transmit, Van Allen Belts.*

TEMPERATURE is a way of telling how hot or cold something is by using a scale of numbers. Two systems of telling TEMPERATURE are Fahrenheit (F) and Celsius or Centigrade (C). Here's how they compare:

	Fahrenheit	Centigrade, Celsius
Boiling	212 degrees	100 degrees
Freezing	32 degrees	0 degrees

Instruments on board a satellite must be kept at a stable TEMPERATURE, because they are damaged by too much heat or cold. Satellites used to be made to rotate so that no one side was overheated by the Sun. Now they're covered with copper or gold foil which reflects much of the heat away and protects them.

A **THERMISTOR** is a tiny instrument the size of a bead. It's fastened to the outside shell or the inside of a satellite. A THERMISTOR measures temperature in outer space. It is an analog computer. See *Analog Computer, Temperature.*

THRUST is the amount of force a rocket has while its fuel is burning. THRUST may be measured in millions of pounds. See *Fuel.*

THRUSTER STEERING When a spacecraft is beyond the Earth's atmosphere, it can be steered with short bursts from small rocket engines called "THRUSTERS" that nudge it one way or another to keep it on course. This is called THRUSTER STEERING. See *Rocket Engine.*

TIROS was a series of weather satellites (1960-64). They sent back pictures of cloud cover and the curvature of the Earth, but it took so long to process the data they sent that they were useless for short-range weather forecasts. They were replaced by the NIMBUS satellites in 1964. See *Data.*

TIROS watches weather, but also helps relay accurate information on distress calls from ships and aircraft equipped with emergency beacons.

To **TRACK** a satellite, one measures its orbit. Has your dog ever sniffed out the path of a cat to where it ran up a tree? That's a kind of cat and dog TRACKING. But satellites don't go up trees. People use telescopes and radar instruments to TRACK a satellite as it travels. See *Radar*.

TRAJECTORY When you throw a rock, the path it takes is its TRAJECTORY. Once a rocket is launched it follows a TRAJECTORY, its path during flight. If a TRAJECTORY repeats itself, it is called an orbit.

To **TRANSMIT** is to send. Usually, TRANSMIT relates to sending information by radio. A television station TRANSMITS sounds and picture information to your television set, or receiver. Earth ground stations TRANSMIT information to satellites and satellites TRANSMIT information to the Earth. See *Communication Satellites, Components, (Ground Stations)*.

U

UNIVERSAL TIME is a system of keeping time based on one spot on the Earth. It counts 24 hours a day without regard to where the Sun is shining on Earth. UNIVERSAL TIME is kept at Greenwich, England. When it's 14 minutes, 16 seconds after the hour at Greenwich, it is 14 minutes, 16 seconds after the hour all around the world, in UNIVERSAL TIME. But Chicago local time might be 14 minutes, 16 seconds after 3 and San Francisco local time would be 14 minutes, 16 seconds after 1. Almost all satellite systems use UNIVERSAL TIME.

The **UNIVERSE** is everything that exists from the atom in a molecule on your big toenail to the farthest star or speck of interstellar dust. The Big Bang theory says that all matter everywhere was once a huge, dense mass that exploded billions of years ago. The result is our UNIVERSE.

The UNIVERSE is also the very last part of your address. You can say, "I am a person who lives on a street, in a city, in a county, in a state, in the United States on the continent of North America in the northern half of the western hemisphere,* on the Earth, in the solar system, in the Milky Way Galaxy, in the UNIVERSE. See *Galaxy, Planet, Solar System.*

---

*You could also say, ". . . the western half of the northern hemisphere."

V

The **VAN ALLEN BELTS** are high-altitude, natural, electomagnetic fields named after Dr. James VAN ALLEN, who identified them. They were discoverd by Explorer 1 in 1958.

The radiation in the BELTS is made up of two kinds of particles: positively-charged protons and negative electrons. Trapped within the Earth's magnetic field, the BELTS extend 50,000 miles thick between the Earth and the Sun. On the side of the Earth away from the Sun, the BELTS are spread by the push of the solar wind to 200,000 miles thick.

In 1962, a nuclear test explosion ejected particles into the solar wind which greatly increased the radiation level of the VAN ALLEN BELTS. This radiation destroyed TELSTAR 1. The astronauts avoid contact with severe radiation by choosing orbits that get around the most intense levels of radiation.

VANGUARD 1 was the fourth satellite ever to be launched. It looked just like a ball. It was six inches in diameter and weighed three pounds. The Americans who launched VANGUARD 1 predict it will orbit the Earth for at least 100 years, maybe even 1000 years. See *Orbit*.

*VIKING lander, photographed on Earth,
but bound for Mars.*

VELOCITY is commonly used as a synonym for *speed*, but is actually the speed in a specific direction. Escape VELOCITY is 7 miles per second *straight up*, while its speed is just 7 miles per second. See *Burnout, Circular Orbit Velocity.*

VIKING The U.S. VIKING 1 and VIKING 2 crafts landed on Mars in 1976. By using radio waves between Mars and Earth to get instructions for their computers, these craft photographed the planet's surface and analyzed its atmosphere and soil. See *Robot.*

VON BRAUN, WERNHER It was in the late 1930s and early 1940s. World War II was about to go into full blast and we do mean blast. In Germany, scientists were thinking up new ways of sending bombs from place to place. WERNHER VON BRAUN worked on the idea of using a rocket to send a bomb to its target. The rocket was called the V-2 and warfare has never been the same since. See *Goddard.*

VOYAGER 1 and 2 satellites aren't really satellites, but they developed out of the same knowledge we use to make satellites. The two VOYAGERS are space robots about the size of compact cars. They were launched late in 1977 and two years later they encountered the planet Jupiter 400 million miles away. These two spacecraft collected over 30,000 images (similar to TV pictures) of Jupiter and its satellites. Both VOYAGERS went on to Saturn, almost 800 million miles from the Earth. Images returning from these craft help scientists to study the rings and satellites of both planets and to learn about their atmospheres, magnetic fields, and weights and densities. See *Atmosphere, Encounter, Images, Robot, Satellite.*

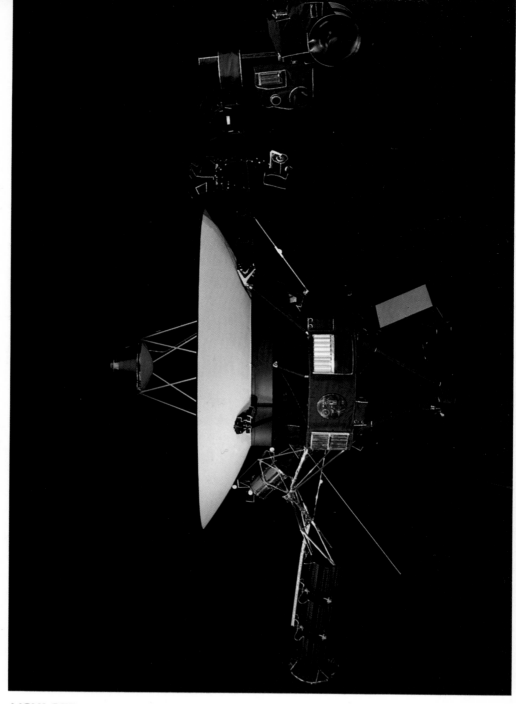

VOYAGER spacecraft designed to explore the planets of our solar system.

W

A **WAVE** is simply a pattern repeated over and over again. Each of the patterns is called a cycle. The length of a cycle is called the wavelength of a WAVE. There are two types of WAVES: standing WAVES and traveling WAVES. If you watch two people twirling a jump rope, you can see what a standing WAVE looks like. You can make a traveling WAVE by putting a long rope on the ground. Shake one end from side to side and the WAVES seem to travel from your end to the other end of the rope.

WEATHER SATELLITES provide information about the ocean, desert, north and south poles, and other areas where weather reports are not easy to get. The first WEATHER SATELLITE, TIROS 1, was launched in April, 1960. Since 1966, the Earth's cloud cover has been photographed at least once daily. These photos locate storm systems, pressure fronts, jet streams, fog, sea ice, and snow cover. They track hurricanes, typhoons, and tropical storms. WEATHER SATELLITES also give useful data for fishing and shipping industries, because their infrared cameras show sea-surface temperatures. NIMBUS, launched in 1962, carried six cameras as well as radiation sensors for heat balance data, temperature, and cloud cover. See *Data, Imaging Equipment.*

WINDOW When you're up at bat playing baseball, there's a WINDOW, a time when it's possible for you to hit the ball. If you swing too soon or too late, you won't hit the ball. You'll just swing and miss it. When a rocket or satellite is being launched to encounter another object in space, there's a launch time WINDOW. If the vehicle is launched too early or too late, the WINDOW is closed. There will be no encounter, just a swing and a miss. See *Encounter.*

Y

YAW is a change in the angle of forward motion that puts a craft off course. See *Attitude, Pitch, Roll.*

Z

The **ZENITH** is straight up. At midday, the Sun is at the ZENITH in the sky, straight overhead. A rocket reaches the ZENITH of its trajectory when it can go no higher and starts to fall back down. See *Rocket, Trajectory.*

Artist's picture of a VOYAGER spacecraft, encountering Saturn.

RUTH AND ED RADLAUER

Shortly after Sputnik I was launched, Ruth and Ed Radlauer began work on a book titled *About Missiles and Men*. Little did they know then that 25 years later they would work on a book telling about satellites mapping the Earth and Moon. The Radlauers take the pictures for most of their books, but they had to let satellites and artists make most of the images found in this book.

The Radlauers, including three adult children, have written over 200 books for people of all ages on subjects that include gymnastics, national parks, drag racing, and coral reefs.

JEAN MATHER

When Jean Mather is not doing her own writing, she is teaching others to write at California State University, Fullerton and Saddleback College. As the mother of young Julie and Michael, she has researched computer camps and published her findings. She also writes technical articles for industrial businesses. Jean volunteers her help at her children's school and in their activity groups, but finds time for herself to do aerobic dancing, skating, baking, and skiing on the snow and in the water whenever possible.

ROBERT E. MATHER

Robert E. Mather, M.B.A., has extensive experience in business computer systems selection and management. He is a partner in M + M Associates which provides independent and unbiased consulting services to business and educational institutions. Bob is involved on a day-to-day basis with the evaluation of computer hardware and software and the design of computer applications for all sizes of computers. Bob is a faculty member of University of California, Irvine, Saddleback College, and is partner in a computer camp for children.